Introduction to the Series

The Unsolved Mysteries library was develo
ies to your classroom. These highly intriguing ...,
and imagination of your students. Each carefully-researched topic presents a balanced view, so the reader can draw his or her own conclusion.

The wide variety of topics in the series will motivate upper elementary, secondary, and adult readers. The low reading levels, ranging from fourth to fifth grade, will encourage student success.

Teaching Strategies

The Teacher's Guide provides easy-to-follow teaching suggestions for each of the books in the series. Each lesson suggests ways to develop and hone comprehension skills while encouraging a sense of pleasure in reading.

Summary provides a synopsis of each book. You may use this summary to familiarize your students and yourself with the mystery.

Background provides a short historical or geographical background of the topic. You may use the information to further familiarize your students and yourself with the topic in general.

Vocabulary provides a list of key words found in the book. These may need to be reviewed before students read the book.

Tapping Prior Knowledge helps prepare and motivate students to read the book. Questions are given that elicit personal responses from students.

Understanding the Book provides literal recall questions that can be discussed after students have read the book. These questions may be used to monitor students' comprehension of the book.

Thinking Critically provides interpretive and evaluative questions. These questions have no right or wrong answers and encourage students to think creatively.

Writing and Extension Activities provides suggestions for activities that may be used to enrich students' understanding of each mystery.

Student Preparation

Before students begin to read this series, explain to them that class discussions will follow each book. To prepare for the discussions, students may wish to take notes on parts of the story they do not understand. They may also want to note aspects of the story they especially like or dislike, any ideas that arise as they are reading, and any words that are unfamiliar. Encourage students to refer to their notes during the discussions. These notes may act as a springboard for further investigation of various elements of the story.

Water Monsters

Vocabulary

You may wish to review these content words with students prior to assigning the book.

serpent

ship's hull

merchant

transatlantic

vast

ship's bridge

port

starboard

expedition

monastery

wreckage

exploit

frolic

outboard motor

emerge

Summary

People in all times and places have claimed to see water monsters. During the eighteenth and nineteenth centuries, many sightings of giant squids and water snakes were recorded by ocean travelers. In the twentieth century, many claimed to have seen monsters in the seas or in large lakes. Some people have made photographs and videotapes, but most of them are not clear. Cryptozoologists, who study these hidden animals, have tried to find and capture water monsters, but without success. Some cryptozoologists believe water monsters are survivors from the time of the dinosaurs, while others think they are just unknown species.

Background

For most of human history, people have sailed the oceans. Early sailors knew little about what lay under the surface. They did know that storms and ocean creatures all too often wrecked their fragile boats. The oceans seemed powerful and mysterious. No wonder the large creatures early sailors saw seemed like monsters bent on their destruction! Today the ocean is still the least thoroughly explored part of the earth, and the unknown creatures who make their homes in the deep still fascinate us.

Tapping Prior Knowledge

The following questions are designed to be used before students read *Water Monsters*. Students' responses will be based on their past experiences, opinions, or knowledge.

1. Suppose someone told you that he or she had seen something unusual, such as a ghost, a UFO, or a monster. Discuss how you would decide whether or not to believe him or her.

2. What would you do if you saw something unusual? How might you try to prove what you saw?

3. Tell about a time when you were frightened by something you thought was a monster or a wild animal. Did you see it clearly? Describe what you saw or heard.

4. What is the biggest animal that you have ever seen? Describe its size in comparison with yourself or with things in the classroom.

Understanding the Book

The following questions are designed to assess students' understanding of important factual information after reading the book.

1. How do we know for sure that the giant squid exists? *(Dead giant squids have washed up on the coast of Canada, and some giant squids have been captured.)*

2. What evidence made people think that French photographer Robert le Serrec's photographs of a sea monster were a trick? *(He was wanted by Interpol, and he left France with money people had given him for an expedition.)*

3. What did scientists think the huge animal caught in the net of a fishing boat off Christchurch, New Zealand, really was? *(Scientists thought it was a basking shark.)*

4. What was Operation Deepscan? *(It was a fleet of motorboats with sound-detection equipment which swept Loch Ness.)*

5. What did the town of Port Henry do to exploit the fame of their water monster? *(People in the town painted their buildings apple green to match the monster, put up a billboard with the names of all the people who had sighted the monster, and sold T-shirts and buttons.)*

6. How did the Native Americans of Lake Okanagan live with their water monster? *(When they had to cross the lake, they threw in live animals to satisfy it.)*

7. Why did scientist Roy Mackal think dinosaurs might survive in the great swamp in the Republic of Congo? *(The swamp was mostly unexplored and resembled what parts of the world had been like in the age of the dinosaurs.)*

8. How does the book say a large creature such as a water monster might find enough food to survive in the small loughs, or lakes, of Connemara? *(A large creature might survive by leaving the water to find food, or by moving from lake to lake.)*

Thinking Critically

The following questions have been developed to promote critical thinking. There are no right or wrong answers to these questions.

1. Do you think the evidence presented in the book proves that water monsters exist? Tell why or why not.
2. How are an animal and a monster the same? How are they different? Make a chart to compare them.
3. Why do you think people find the idea of water monsters so appealing?
4. Do you think it is important to find out whether water monsters are real? Should scientists study the creatures if they can be found, or should water monsters remain a mystery? Explain your reasons.
5. What reasons might someone have to try to fool people into believing that they had seen water monsters? What benefits might such a person expect?
6. Some people think that water monsters might be dinosaurs. Do you agree or disagree? What evidence does the book give to support this possibility?

Writing and Extension Activities

Choose from among the following activities to enrich students' understanding of the book. You may wish to select separate activities for students of different abilities and interests or to assign an activity as a group project.

1. Have students design traps for water monsters. Then have each student present his or her design to the class in the form of a sketch or model.
2. Suggest that students write a fictional account of a sighting of a water monster or mythological creature, such as a dragon or a unicorn. Remind students to include sensory details to make their account realistic.
3. Encourage students to research the depth, flora, and fauna of Lake Champlain. Then ask them to make a poster showing an area of the lake which might provide a good habitat for a water monster.
4. Ask students how they would go about searching for a water monster. What equipment would they use? Ask students to make a plan for an expedition.
5. Today many people believe that animals have rights. Ask students what rights water monsters might have. Have them create a water monsters' bill of rights.
6. If students are interested in finding out more about what it would be like to sail the seas and see the strange creatures of the deep, suggest they search for books in the library under *oceanography, seas,* or *sailing.*
7. Encourage students to write a story about one of the incidents in the book from the monster's point of view.

The Mysteries of UFOs

Vocabulary

You may wish to review these content words with students prior to assigning the book.

- wreckage
- transport plane
- missile range
- debris
- incident
- code name
- conventional
- dismiss a possibility
- missionary
- shaft of light
- enthusiast
- bureau
- vertically
- exhaust
- physicist

Summary

A wave of UFO sightings began in 1947, when Kenneth Arnold saw something that he described as flying like a saucer skipping across water. After newspapers printed stories of "flying saucers," reports flooded in. In 1952, the Air Force created Project Blue Book to investigate UFO sightings, but the Project did not prove or disprove the existence of UFOs. Many descriptions of UFOs resemble experimental aircraft, but some people claim that the crafts they have seen were carrying visitors from outer space.

Background

Has Earth been visited by beings from outer space? Many people think that is the explanation for strange objects they have seen in the sky. For some, the idea that technically advanced beings are visiting our planet is frightening. These people think that the intentions of the visitors are harmful to us. Others think that the visitors are friendly and might be able to help us solve some of Earth's global problems like pollution. Perhaps some day humans will have such powerful technology that we can visit other planets. Then we would be the ones in the UFOs!

Tapping Prior Knowledge

The following questions are designed to be used before students read *The Mysteries of UFOs*. Students' responses will be based on their past experiences, feelings, or knowledge.

1. Tell about a time that you saw something in the sky that you could not identify. What did it look like? Did someone else know what it was? What did it turn out to be?
2. Describe a UFO sighting that you have read about or heard about. What happened? What did the eyewitnesses claim to have seen?

3. If UFOs really exist, what do you think they might look like? Do you think they come in different sizes and colors? Explain why you think so.
4. Name as many different types of aircraft as you can. Describe the shape, size, and color of those you have seen. Do you think any of these could be mistaken for a UFO? Why or why not?

Understanding the Book

The following questions are designed to assess students' understanding of important factual information after reading the book.

1. How was the name "flying saucers" invented? *(Kenneth Arnold described strange objects he saw from his own small plane as flying like a saucer would if you skipped it across the water.)*
2. How did witnesses describe the alien bodies they claimed to see in a wreck near the White Sands missile range? *(Witnesses said the aliens had large, round heads, small, strangely-spaced eyes, and no hair.)*
3. What did Air Force Brigadier-General Roger Ramey say that the wreckage found by Mac Brazel in the Roswell Incident really was? *(Ramey said it was a weather balloon.)*
4. What did people see in the skies above Nuremberg, Germany, and Basel, Switzerland, in the sixteenth century? *(They saw two huge black tubes, out of which came blue, black, and red balls, blood-red crosses, and disk shapes.)*
5. What were the "foo fighters" seen by pilots in Word War II? *(The "foo fighters" were balls of light that appeared out of nowhere and seemed to play with the airplanes, diving and darting in the sky around them.)*
6. What illness did Betty Cash, Vickie Landrum, and Vickie's young grandson Colby develop after seeing a UFO? *(They developed radiation sickness.)*
7. What did missionary Reverend William Gill and his companions see in the sky in Papua, New Guinea? *(They saw men come out of a circular aircraft onto a narrower upper deck and wave at them.)*

Thinking Critically

The following questions have been developed to promote critical thinking. There are no right or wrong answers to these questions.

1. Why do you think many people refused to believe that the wreckage involved in the Roswell Incident was the remains of the weather balloons from Project Mogul?
2. How might you explain the colored balls seen in the skies above Nuremberg, Germany, and Basel, Switzerland?
3. Why do you think there are so few authenticated photographs of UFOs?

4. Do you believe that the glowing red object a jet bomber pilot chased for 700 miles was a passenger plane? Why or why not?
5. Do you think that UFO sightings get too much, not enough, or the right amount of attention they deserve? Why do you think as you do?
6. Do you think Betty Cash and Vickie Landrum had a good case in their lawsuit against the U.S. government? Tell why or why not.
7. Do you think most UFO sightings are really sightings of secret experimental aircraft? Why or why not?

Writing and Extension Activities

Choose from among the following activities to enrich students' understanding of the book. You may wish to select separate activities for students of different abilities and interests or to assign an activity as a group project.

1. Encourage students to watch the sky for 15 minutes a day for a week and keep a journal of anything unusual they see. Have them share their journals with the class.
2. Suggest that students search their local library's card catalog using the keywords "aircraft" and "military" to find out more about experimental aircraft. Have students report their findings to the class.
3. Have students write a story about a real or imaginary UFO sighting. Collect all the stories in a notebook or binder. Give the collection a name.
4. Encourage students to think about the best way to signal aliens aboard a UFO. Have students share their UFO communication plans with the class.
5. Have students design a landing strip for alien UFOs. Make sure they think about what sorts of food and fuel the aliens will need, and how to keep them from being mobbed by curious humans. Have students share their plans with the class.
6. Suggest that students make drawings of UFOs. Have them refer to the book or to other resources for information. Display the drawings in the classroom.
7. Encourage students to write their ideas for the plot of a movie about UFOs. Have students share or perform their ideas.
8. Have students think about ways that people might protect themselves from UFOs. Have them list the items in their UFO defense kit. Discuss the lists with the class.

Alien Visitors and Abductions

Vocabulary

civilian

fluid

state of shock

radar

navigation

intruder

descend

infirm

hover

emerge

heliport

device

paralyze

subconscious

Summary

Since the 1940s, people have reported seeing UFOs. In the 1960s, people around the world began making claims that they had been abducted by aliens. Most of these people did not remember being abducted until they were hypnotized. Some people say they have photographed aliens or their ships, but none of these photos have proved genuine. As humans have explored more of the solar system, speculation about the origin of the alleged aliens has moved farther from Earth. This fact, combined with the similarity of stories about aliens with old myths about goblins and leprechauns makes it seem likely that aliens are a modern myth.

Background

Aliens appear to be a popular topic today. We see them on TV, in movies, in books, and even in some types of magazines and newspapers. Many people are anxious to believe in aliens, perhaps wishing to find greater wisdom and knowledge or to acquire the marvelous powers attributed to aliens. Other people are quick to dismiss the possibility of alien existence, explaining mysterious alien-like happenings with scientific research.

Tapping Prior Knowledge

The following questions are designed to be used before students read *Alien Visitors and Abductions*. Students' responses will be based on their past experiences, opinions, or knowledge.

1. Some people claim to have seen UFOs, but their sightings turn out to be jets, helicopters, weather balloons, or shooting stars. How do you think these objects are alike and different from UFOs?

2. Tell about an alien story that you have read in a book, magazine, or tabloid newspaper. Did you find the story believable? Why or why not?
3. Tell what aliens have been like in the movies you have seen. Were they friendly or dangerous? What were their physical characteristics?
4. What would you do if you saw an alien? Would you be curious, afraid, or both? How would you communicate with the alien?
5. If you could go to another planet, which one would you visit? What do you think you might see there?

Understanding the Book

The following questions are designed to assess students' understanding of important factual information after reading the book.

1. What clue led Betty and Barney Hill and others to think they may have been abducted, even though they didn't remember it happening? *(There was a period of time they couldn't account for. In the Hills' case, they got home two hours after they should have.)*
2. What two facts made people doubt the story told by Antonio Villas Boas, the Brazilian who identified himself as a farmer? *(Boas was really a lawyer, and he had not needed hypnosis to remember his abduction.)*
3. What did the Air Force investigation into the Roswell Incident claim that the "metallic, disk-shaped object" seen by Grady Barnett was? *(The Air Force said it was a special balloon designed to keep an eye on Soviet nuclear testing.)*
4. How was George Adamski's claim that he had visited the moon on a alien spacecraft disproved? *(Space exploration showed that the surface of the moon did not match Adamski's description.)*
5. What event seemed to fulfill the prediction Orfeo Angelucci said that the Space Brothers made about something terrible happening in 1986? *(There was an accident at the Soviet nuclear power plant at Chernobyl.)*
6. How have most witnesses described aliens? *(Most witnesses have described them as small beings with large heads, catlike eyes, and silvery coveralls.)*
7. What was discovered about the clear photographs of alien spacecraft taken by Swiss farmer Eduard Meier? *(A computer test showed that they were hoaxes.)*
8. What mythical beings do aliens resemble? *(Aliens resemble goblins, leprechauns, and pixies.)*

Thinking Critically

The following questions have been developed to promote critical thinking. There are no right or wrong answers to these questions.

1. Do you think the evidence presented in this book proves that aliens really visit the earth? Tell why or why not.
2. Do you think hypnosis always produces an accurate account of events? Tell why or why not.
3. Why do you think most people who claimed to be abducted could only remember their abductions under hypnosis?
4. If aliens were abducting people and performing medical tests on them, what might they be trying to find out?
5. Do you think it is possible to mistake a wrecked weather balloon or satellite for a UFO? Tell why or why not.
6. Why do you think so many different people give similar accounts of alien abductions?

Writing and Extension Activities

Choose from among the following activities to enrich students' understanding of the book. You may wish to select separate activities for students of different abilities and interests or to assign an activity as a group project.

1. Ask students what they would like to ask or say to an alien if they ever met one. Suggest that they write a list of questions and statements.
2. Ask students what they think the policy of the United States toward alien visitors should be. Suggest they write a statement of policy.
3. Ask students what planet they would like most to visit. Encourage each student to research his or her planet and write a fictional account of a trip to that planet.
4. Suggest that students choose objects to be placed in a "time capsule." Explain that the objects should tell aliens about life on Earth.
5. Discuss with students what it might be like to live in outer space for an extended period of time. Have students work in groups to design livable space stations. Encourage them to read about life on the space station Mir.
6. Ask students to pretend that they are from another planet, either real or imaginary. Have them write and illustrate travel brochures encouraging tourists to visit.
7. Encourage students to write about their favorite activity (such as a sport, game, or dance) from the point of view of an alien.
8. Have students imagine that they are going to open a hotel for alien visitors. What furnishings will they need? What food will they serve? Ask students to write a few paragraphs about their alien hotel.

Where was Atlantis?

Vocabulary

peninsula

extensive

survey

joint

chariot

variations

monument

asunder

material evidence

relic

meditation

ore

dramatic

site

occupation

Summary

In the late 19th century, people became interested in the story of Atlantis written by the ancient Greek philosopher Plato. People developed many theories about the location of Atlantis and the nature of its civilization, but none of them were able to prove their theories. Experts now believe that Atlantis was really the Mediterranean island of Crete, which was an early center of civilization. Crete was destroyed by tidal waves and volcanic ash from the explosion of a nearby island.

Background

Most cultures in history have looked back to a "golden age" when life was supposed to have been easy. People in the Judeo-Christian tradition believe that humans began in the Garden of Eden, but were cast out for disobedience. The tendency of people to idealize the past may explain how memories of the rich and sophisticated culture of Minoan Crete might have been transformed into the legend of Atlantis.

Tapping Prior Knowledge

The following questions are designed to be used before students read *Where was Atlantis?* Students' responses will be based on their past experiences, opinions, or knowledge.

1. Tell about a place you have visited that is very different from your home town. What did you hear or read about this place before you went? How did the place compare with what you had heard about it?
2. Have you ever heard stories of a place where everyone was happy and there were no problems? Did you believe that the place was real? Tell why or why not.

3. Discuss a natural disaster such as a flood, tornado, volcano, or earthquake. What do you think it would be like to live through such a disaster? Think of adjectives to describe what you might see.

4. Have you ever talked with an older person about what life was like when they were young? Tell about the differences and similarities between life now and life then.

5. Tell about a book that you have read or a television program that you have seen about life long ago. What were some of the things about life in past times that seemed strange to you? What were some of the similarities to your life?

Understanding the Book

The following questions are designed to assess students' understanding of important factual information after reading the book.

1. Who gave the first written account of Atlantis? *(The first written account of Atlantis was given by the Greek philosopher Plato.)*

2. What did Plato say happened to the continent of Atlantis? *(Plato said that violent earthquakes and floods caused Atlantis to be swallowed by the sea.)*

3. What continent did early explorers mistake for Atlantis? *(Early explorers thought America was Atlantis.)*

4. What giant structures found in Egypt and Central America led Igantius Donnelly to think that civilizations in both places were descended from the civilization of Atlantis? *(The pyramids of Egypt and Central America are roughly similar in shape, perhaps showing a common origin.)*

5. What real island do most experts now believe was Atlantis? *(Most experts now believe that Crete was Atlantis.)*

6. What did Sir Arthur Evans find on Crete that made him think the myth of the Minotaur might have been based on truth? *(Evans found a magnificent palace with wall paintings showing men and women leaping over a charging bull.)*

7. How was Minoan Crete destroyed? *(The volcanic island Thera exploded, causing tidal waves that hit Crete and covered it with volcanic ash.)*

Thinking Critically

The following questions have been developed to promote critical thinking. There are no right or wrong answers to these questions.

1. What do you think the appearance of pyramids on different continents proves? Do you think it shows that people on different continents had contact with one another or that they just happened to build similar structures? Explain why you think so.

2. Most myths and legends are based on at least a little bit of truth. Tell why you think this is true. How do you think the truth gets stretched?

3. How could an entire island or continent sink into the sea in a single night? Do you think it could have really happened that way? Tell why or why not.

4. Describe what you know about the work of an archaeologist. Do you think it would be exciting to be an archaeologist? Tell why or why not.

5. Could a natural disaster destroy our civilization as it did Minoan Crete? Tell why or why not. What type of natural disaster do you think it would be?

6. What are some ways that older civilizations have influenced the customs where you live? Name some ways in which plants, animals, metals such as gold, statues, and buildings were used in the same ways then as now.

Writing and Extension Activities

Choose from among the following activities to enrich students' understanding of the book. You may wish to select separate activities for students of different abilities and interests or to assign an activity as a group project.

1. Suggest that students draw a map of Atlantis. Encourage them to refer to the book for details of the city's plan.

2. Ask students to write a fictional travel guide for Atlantis. Remind them to include information on things to do and see.

3. Encourage students to imagine the perfect city. Then have them write a short description of one of the features of that city.

4. Suggest that students use a library to research the Minoan civilization. Then ask them to report their findings to the class.

5. Ask students to imagine that they are in charge of public safety in Atlantis. What plans might they have made to save the people of Atlantis from disaster?

6. Encourage students to write a fictional account of a tidal wave or volcanic eruption. Remind students to refer to the book or another resource for details of these natural disasters.

7. Encourage students to plan an archaeological dig of an area in their town. What might they expect to find? Refer students to an encyclopedia for information on archaeological methods.

8. Ask students what period of history they would visit if they had a time machine. Encourage students to write a story about a trip to this time.

Mysteries of the Ancients

Vocabulary

You may wish to review these content words with students prior to assigning the book.

- ancient
- natives
- stone figures
- burial grounds
- chisel
- pillar
- idol
- courtyard
- ornament
- upheaval
- chamber
- invade
- occupy a country
- engineer
- gilded

Summary

All over the world there are clues to ancient civilizations. There are huge statues on Easter Island in the Pacific, a magnificent stone city in the Andes Mountains of Bolivia, and giant pyramids in Egypt. From the sixteenth century to the present day, people have searched South America for the legendary city of El Dorado. Archaeologists are still trying to solve the mysteries of these fabulous legends and magnificent ruins.

Background

As civilizations have grown, humans throughout the world have developed a variety of cultures. Some of these were similar to our culture today, and some were very different. Some left records that we can read, and others did not. Archaeologists help us learn about past civilizations by studying the buildings and other artifacts they left. They use delicate instruments to carefully uncover ancient bones, plant seeds, tools, and pottery from early civilizations. They have also found large structures used hundreds of years ago, such as buildings, tombs, and canals. Some archaeologists even work underwater.

Tapping Prior Knowledge

The following questions are designed to be used before students read *Mysteries of the Ancients*. Students' responses will be based on their past experiences, opinions, or knowledge.

1. Discuss a television program you have seen or a book or article you have read about a civilization from long ago. What did you learn about that civilization? In what ways did the lives of its people seem strange or familiar to you?

2. Describe what pictures come to your mind when you think about the word *ancient*. If you have ever seen a picture of an ancient ruin, tell what it looked like and what you learned about it. Then discuss the difference between something that is ancient and something that is just old.
3. Tell about items you have seen in a museum that came from an ancient civilization. Did you find it easy or difficult to tell what the things were and how they were used?

Understanding the Book
The following questions are designed to assess students' understanding of important factual information after reading the book.

1. How did Easter Island get its name? *(A Dutch sailor, Jacob Roggeveen, first saw it on Easter Sunday.)*
2. Why did Thor Heyerdahl sail across the Pacific Ocean on a raft? *(Heyerdahl wanted to show that people from South America could have reached the Pacific Islands.)*
3. What did Atan say the red hats on the heads of some of the Easter Island statues represented? *(Atan said they represented topknots of red hair.)*
4. Why did many Europeans believe that Tiahuanaco could not have been built by the local people? *(Many Europeans believed the local people could not have made such large buildings.)*
5. What facts support the theory that Tiahuanaco is the last remnant of the lost civilization of Atlantis, which was supposed to have sunk beneath the sea? *(Lake Titicaca, a salt-water lake that once reached to the city, might once have been connected with the ocean, and the ruins of an ancient seaport were found near Tiahuanaco.)*
6. How were the pyramids probably built? *(Blocks of stone were probably pushed up huge ramps of earth on wooden rollers.)*
7. For what purpose might the Great Pyramid have been used before it was completed? *(The Great Pyramid might have been used as an observatory.)*
8. Why was the ruler of an ancient South American city called El Dorado? *(The ruler was called El Dorado, the gilded one, because every year he covered his body with gold dust and jumped into a nearby lake.)*

Thinking Critically
The following questions have been developed to promote critical thinking. There are no right or wrong answers to these questions.

1. Do you think the Easter Island statues could all have been raised in the way demonstrated by Atan? Tell why or why not, explaining other ways you think they could have been raised.

2. For what purpose do you think the lifelike statues described by the Spanish visitor to Tiahuanaco were made? Why do you think so?

3. Do you think Tiahuanaco could be a part of the lost civilization of Atlantis? Why or why not?

4. For what purpose do you think the Great Pyramid was built? Explain your reasoning. If you built a pyramid today, how would you use it?

5. What do you think happened to Colonel Fawcett, his son, and his friend on their search for El Dorado? Why do you think so?

6. Some people think that El Dorado will still be found. Discuss why you agree or disagree with this possibility.

Writing and Extension Activities

Choose from among the following activities to enrich students' understanding of the book. You may wish to select separate activities for students of different abilities and interests or to assign an activity as a group project.

1. Encourage students to imagine that future archaeologists couldn't read our languages. Have them write a report showing what a future archaeologist could tell about our civilization from exploring their school buildings.

2. Suggest that students write a poem about an Easter Island statue, a pyramid, or a ruined stone city. Gather the poems together in a notebook or binder, and have the class decide on a name for the collection.

3. Suggest that students write stories set in ancient times on Easter Island, in South America, or in Egypt. Have students check the details of the settings by using encyclopedias or other books.

4. Have students invent their own written language using pictographs or symbols like the ones some ancient people used. Encourage them to draw sentences with their symbols and have other students try to tell what they mean.

5. Encourage students to make a list of things they would take on an archaeological expedition to an ancient ruin. If they need guidance, have them read about archaeology in an encyclopedia or in other resources.

6. Suggest that students make a list of items they think should be included in a time capsule to tell future archaeologists about our civilization.

7. Encourage students to think about the best characteristics of their home town. Then ask them to write a description of the town that might make a future explorer curious to find out more.

Ghosts of Flight 401

Vocabulary

You may wish to review these content words with students prior to assigning the book.

flight engineer

mentally alert

embankment

supervisor

flight deck

public address system

food catering

trap door

compartment

stall in flight

to salvage

porthole

work shift

airship

leakage

Summary

On December 29, 1972, Eastern Airlines Flight 401 crashed into the Everglades. After the crash, parts saved from the wreckage were used in other planes. On some of these planes, passengers and crew members began reporting sightings of the dead crew of the crashed plane. Sometimes these ghosts gave warnings about things that were about to go wrong. Eventually these sightings stopped. Some people claim to have had psychic contact with the victims of other air disasters as well.

Background

The Federal Aviation Administration sets very strict rules for how thoroughly planes must be checked and how often. A commercial passenger jet must have a thorough maintenance check and oil change after every 100 hours of flight time, with somewhat simpler checks performed after every 50 flight hours. There is also an extensive list of items that must be checked before every take-off, which is done by the pilots and ground crew. These checkpoints include tests for air pressure in the tires, movement and pressure in the brakes and flaps, and overall weight and load balance. The pilots also check their instruments, test the controls, look for problems indicated in the control panels, and check engine throttle, radio frequencies, and brakes.

Tapping Prior Knowledge

The following questions are designed to be used before students read *Ghosts of Flight 401*. Students' responses will be based on their past experiences, opinions, or knowledge.

1. Some people claim to have strange feelings that something bad is about to happen. Tell about a time you may have felt this way and what happened afterward.

2. Tell about a time that you saw something in the dark that startled or frightened you. What did it turn out to be? How did you react?
3. Discuss a news article or book you have read about ghosts. Did you believe that the ghosts described were real? Why or why not?
4. What do you like best about flying somewhere in a jet? If you have never flown before, do you think you would like to? Why or why not?

Understanding the Book

The following questions are designed to assess students' understanding of important factual information after reading the book.

1. What did Dorothy E. imagine seeing in her vision? *(She imagined seeing the left wing of a plane break up and the plane crash to the ground.)*
2. How did Captain Loft accidentally turn off the plane's autopilot? *(He must have pressed on the steering column as he leaned over to help Stockstill change a light bulb.)*
3. What did Virginia see near plane #318 that seemed to be causing the plane to roll to the right? *(She saw a hazy mass hovering over the right wingtip.)*
4. What did a female passenger on a TWA plane landing in Phoenix, Arizona, see that made her begin to scream uncontrollably? *(She saw a man suddenly appear in the seat next to her and then vanish.)*
5. What warning did the ghost of Don Repo seem to give the crew of a plane flying to Mexico City? *(The ghost seemed to tell them to watch out for fire on the plane.)*
6. What serious faults were found in the airship R101 when it was first tested? *(Its framework and its engines were too heavy, and the gas bags rubbed against the inside of the framework, causing leaks.)*
7. What did the psychic Eileen Garrett say caused the crash of the British airship R101? *(She said that the added middle section was too heavy for the power of the engines.)*
8. Why have some people suggested that the spirits of people who die suddenly might appear as ghosts? *(They believe that the spirits of the dead are anxious about unfinished business.)*

Thinking Critically

The following questions have been developed to promote critical thinking. There are no right or wrong answers to these questions.

1. Do you believe in ghosts? Why or why not?
2. Do you think that psychic visions might be real, like the one in which Dorothy E. predicted the crash of Flight 401? Why or why not?

3. How might someone who doesn't believe in ghosts explain airline passengers and crews seeing vanishing men who looked like the dead crew of Flight 401?

4. Why do you think the management of Eastern Airlines denied that there had been any reports of ghosts?

5. Why do you think ground maintenance crews were ordered to remove all the parts from the crashed plane from other planes in which they had been used?

6. Do you believe that "psychometry," picking up on sensations and emotions connected with an object, is possible? Why or why not?

7. What tests might the crew have done on the airship R101 to see if it was safe?

8. Why do you think some people rushed the completion of airship R101?

Writing and Extension Activities

Choose from among the following activities to enrich students' understanding of the book. You may wish to select separate activities for students of different abilities and interests or to assign an activity as a group project.

1. Suggest that students look for books of ghost stories in the library. Ask each student to read a book. Then have a class discussion about ghosts.

2. Encourage students to use an encyclopedia or other library resource to find out the duties of each member of an airline crew.

3. Suggest students write an adventure story about an airplane passenger who survives a fiery crash. Ask students to share their stories with the class.

4. Suggest that students write a ghost story. Ask students to share their stories with the class.

5. Have students use their library's periodical catalog to look up predictions for the coming year that were made last New Year. Ask them to count and see how many of the predictions came true.

6. Encourage students to write an account of a recent event from the point of view of someone who has passed away. Tell students to assume that the dead person can hear and see everything.

7. Have students think creatively to design a method for switching off an airplane's autopilot in case of emergency. Have them share their designs with the class.

8. Suggest that students search their library's card catalog, as well as an encyclopedia, to find out more about the job done by air traffic controllers. Have students report their findings to the class.

Giant Humanlike Beasts

Vocabulary

You may wish to review these content words with students prior to assigning the book.

expedition

region

science academy

army unit

species

preserve

prehistoric

roam

descendant

stride

deserted

animated

origin

substance

plaster cast

Summary

For years, people in the Himalayas, China, Central Asia, and North America have sighted animals that looked like large, hairy humans. Some people have taken pictures and videos of the beasts, and others have made casts of their footprints. Some experts believe that these creatures are descendants of Neanderthals, a type of prehistoric humans.

Background

Animals that live in extremely cold climates have physical characteristics that help them survive harsh, freezing temperatures. For example, polar bears have very dense fur all over their bodies. The fur is so thick that they can even go for a swim in icy water. They also have a thick layer of fat that helps insulate them from cold winds. Perhaps these characteristics explain why some people think that the giant, human-like, furry creatures of certain cold mountain regions are really unknown species of bears.

Tapping Prior Knowledge

The following questions are designed to be used before students read Giant Humanlike Beasts. Students' responses will be based on their past experiences, opinions, or knowledge.

1. Tell about a story you have read or a television show you have seen that described Bigfoot or a similar beast. Did you find the report believable? Why or why not?
2. Discuss what you know about the earliest humans. Where did they live? What did they eat? What tools did they use?
3. List what you know about bears. Then list what you know about large apes. Describe how each animal looks, how they move, and where they live. Then compare them to how humans look, move, and live.

4. Animals don't use human languages, but they have their own systems of communication. What animals have you communicated with? Tell how you talked with the animals and how you knew what they needed or wanted.

Understanding the Book

The following questions are designed to assess students' understanding of important factual information after reading the book.

1. What did Captain d'Auvergne say a yeti did for him in a snow storm in the Himalayas? *(Captain d'Auvergne said the yeti carried him to a cave and fed him until he was able to walk again.)*

2. What did the Abominable Snowman Expedition organized by the Daily Mail in 1954 find? *(The expedition only found some vague tracks in the snow.)*

3. To what animal did Dr. Guoxing believe the preserved hands and feet that he was sent belonged? *(Dr. Guoxing believed they belonged to a monkey.)*

4. What animal did the anthropologist Pei Wen Xung believe the Wildman of China really was? *(He believed the Wildman was the descendant of a pre-historic ape called Gigantopithecus.)*

5. What did the Kazakh herdsman tell Khaklov he had seen a female Alma eat? *(He said she ate raw meat, some vegetables and grain, and sometimes insects that she caught.)*

6. What origin did Professor Porshev suggest for the Almas in his article in Current Anthropology? *(He suggested that they were the descendants of Neanderthals.)*

7. Why was William Roe unable to shoot the Bigfoot he spotted? *(He was unable to shoot it because it was so humanlike.)*

8. How did Professor Stringer think it might be possible to prove that Neanderthals had not died out? *(He thought it might be possible to compare DNA from the bones of Neanderthals with living people to see if they were partly descended from Neanderthals.)*

Thinking Critically

The following questions have been developed to promote critical thinking. There are no right or wrong answers to these questions.

1. Do you think the evidence in this book proves that giant humanlike beasts really exist? Tell why or why not.

2. If scientists were to discover where giant humanlike beasts lived, what do you think they should do, and why?

3. Why do you think someone might pretend to have seen a giant humanlike beast? What might the person hope to gain?

4. What are some differences between animals and humans? To which group do you think giant humanlike beasts belong, and why?
5. Why do you think people from different parts of the world give similar accounts of giant humanlike beasts?
6. Do you think it is possible for someone to mistake a bear or other animal for a giant humanlike beast? Tell why or why not.
7. Should people leave some parts of the world more or less unexplored, or should we learn about every part of our planet and all the creatures who live there? Tell why you think so.

Writing and Extension Activities

Choose from among the following activities to enrich students' understanding of the book. You may wish to select separate activities for students of different abilities and interests or to assign an activity as a group project.

1. Ask students to imagine that they have adopted a Bigfoot. What would they teach the creature to help it fit into modern society?
2. Suggest that students write a story from the point of view of a Bigfoot or other humanlike beast who had seen a group of people.
3. Encourage students to imagine what it would be like to live as a Bigfoot, far from towns and other conveniences. Have them make a list of the things they would need to survive.
4. Suggest that students make their own "cave drawings" on paper with charcoal. Remind students to think about what things early humans would have seen in the world around them.
5. Ask students to write a proposal to the United States Congress for a Bigfoot reservation. Remind students to think of reasons to persuade legislators that land should be set aside for the Bigfoot.
6. Encourage students to imagine what humans might be like in thousands of years. Ask them to write a description of present-day man from the point of view of one of these later humans.
7. Suggest that students write a plan for an expedition to look for giant humanlike beasts. Have them include where they would go, a list of what they would need, and a plan of how they would search.
8. Ask students what they would say to a giant humanlike beast if they ever met one. How would they make sure that it could understand them? How could they use written messages to help?

The **Bermuda Triangle**

Vocabulary

You may wish to review these content words with students prior to assigning the book.

torpedo

moorings

cargo

navigation

cadet

gale

smuggler

civil organization

aviation

military base

certificate

seabed

buoy

dimension of space

mineral

Summary

In a 1964 magazine article, Vincent Gaddis coined the term "The Bermuda Triangle." He claimed that this was an area in which ships and airplanes often disappeared. Others adopted Gaddis's idea, and many strange events were reported in the area. Some writers think that the Bermuda Triangle is a place where space and time are distorted, or where another dimension meets our own. However, most of the disappearances that have happened in the Bermuda Triangle have ordinary explanations. There is no proof that anything unusual is happening there.

Background

Hurricanes in the Bermuda Triangle occur mostly during the peak storm months of August and September, when the water temperatures are very warm and the air is moist. Lasting from a few days to two weeks, the winds swirling around the eye of a hurricane can reach speeds of almost 200 miles per hour. The fierce winds, heavy rains, sudden flooding, and huge waves crashing against coastlines cause a great deal of damage to land, ocean vessels, and even airplanes.

Tapping Prior Knowledge

The following questions are designed to be used before students read *The Bermuda Triangle*. Students' responses will be based on their past experiences, opinions, or knowledge.

1. What do you know about the Bermuda Triangle? How did you hear about it? Tell what you know about this area of the Atlantic Ocean.
2. Tell about a time you have been on an airplane or on a boat or ship. What was it like? If you have not been on an airplane, boat, or ship, tell which one you would rather ride on and why.

3. Some reports have been told of airplanes and ships that have disappeared in the Bermuda Triangle. What did you think might have happened?

4. Certain areas of the Atlantic Ocean and other large bodies of water have several hurricanes and other fierce storms each year. Tell about a time that you or someone you know have been in a terrible storm. What did you do for safety? How did you feel during and after the storm?

Understanding the Book

The following questions are designed to assess students' understanding of important factual information after reading the book.

1. Why did the people who found the abandoned Mary Celeste think it was unlikely that the ship had been attacked by thieves or pirates? (The cargo had not been stolen.)

2. Why couldn't the mystery of the Mary Celeste have happened in the Bermuda Triangle? (The Mary Celeste was found more than 3,000 miles east of Bermuda.)

3. What crews of ships thought to be missing in the Bermuda Triangle were rescued? (The crews of the fishing boat John and Mary and the yacht La Dahama were rescued.)

4. What did secret German records show had probably happened to the Proteus? (Records show that the Proteus was probably sunk by a German submarine.)

5. What did the Coast Guard say probably happened to the Rubicon, which was found with the crew's belongings and a dog still on board? (The Coast Guard said the Rubicon had probably broken free from its moorings when a hurricane struck Havana.)

6. What did surviving crew members say about the vanishing of the Southern Isles? (The crew members said that the ship suddenly broke in half and sank so quickly that there was no chance of sending a radio message for help.)

7. What did the Navy say about the purpose of Project Magnet? (The Navy said that the purpose of Project Magnet was to make new maps of all the oceans of the world.)

8. What natural events might make the area of the Bermuda Triangle dangerous? (Frequent hurricanes might make the area dangerous.)

Thinking Critically

The following questions have been developed to promote critical thinking. There are no right or wrong answers to these questions.

1. What is your guess about the disappearance of the five Avenger bombers? Do you think UFOs had anything to do with it? Why or why not?

2. What do you think happened to the captain and crew of the Mary Celeste? Why do you think so?

3. If you were the captain of a ship and heard a weather report of a hurricane coming, what would you do to keep the ship and passengers safe? How would you feel?

4. Do you think that old ships in fair condition should be allowed to transport cargo across the Atlantic Ocean? What about taking passengers?

5. If Donald Crowhurst abandoned his trimaran, why do you think he might have done so? What else might explain what happened to him?

6. Do you think there is a great mystery about things that happen in the Bermuda Triangle, or do you think there is a scientific explanation for everything that happens there? Explain your thinking.

7. How would you explain the lost time that Bruce Gernon Jr. experienced while flying through a tunnel-shaped cloud?

Writing and Extension Activities

Choose from among the following activities to enrich students' understanding of the book. You may wish to select separate activities for students of different abilities and interests or to assign an activity as a group project.

1. Encourage students to use the keywords Bermuda Triangle to search their library's periodical index. Have students read one of the articles they find and report on it to the class.

2. Suggest that students write a story about what they think happened to the Mary Celeste. Make sure students use the facts given in the book.

3. Have students refer to the book to mark the Bermuda Triangle on a copy of a map. Then ask students to find approximately where the Mary Celeste was when it was discovered.

4. Suggest that students write a fictional first-person account of someone whose ship or plane has disappeared in the Bermuda Triangle. Encourage students to imagine what might happen to the person after the disappearance. Have students share their accounts with the class.

5. Encourage students to use an encyclopedia or other resource to find out more about storms in the Atlantic Ocean. Have students report their findings to the class.

6. Suggest that students write an outline of a movie about a ship or airplane that runs into a storm at sea. Have students list which actors and actresses they would like to be in their movie.

7. Have students write a song about the disappearance of one of the ships mentioned in the book. Then ask volunteers to perform their songs.

The **Cosmic Joker**

Vocabulary

You may wish to review these content words with students prior to assigning the book.

civilization

manuscript

psychic

attract

alien

cosmic

bizarre

coincidence

suburb

coronation

assassin

carpentry

tragedy

complex

impact

Summary

Almost every culture in the world has stories about a powerful figure that plays tricks on human beings. In the stories that are told, some tricksters are people and others are animals. In the past century, some people have written theories that a mysterious force, nicknamed the Cosmic Joker, causes strange things to happen. They credit this joker with bizarre weather events and weird coincidences, but scientists do not agree. Scientists and mathematicians are currently working on theories which may explain more facts about these mysterious occurrences.

Background

Stories have been written for centuries concerning objects seeming to fall from the skies. Certain children's books have told about falling skies that turned out to be acorns dropping from a tree or falling meatballs that turned out to be imaginations about rain. A great number of factual articles and books have also been written about objects that fall from the sky. Astronomers have studied and written about meteors that fall, sometimes called shooting stars. Meteorologists tell us about weather conditions on Earth, including predicting when rain, sleet, hail, and snow might fall.

Tapping Prior Knowledge

The following questions are designed to be used before students read The Cosmic Joker. Students' responses will be based on their past experiences, opinions, or knowledge.

1. Tell about a book you have read that was about something strange falling from the sky, something unusual in the sky, or about a strange coincidence. Was the book fiction or nonfiction? How did you know?

2. What is the strangest happening that you have heard about or read about? Describe what happened.

3. What do you know about twins and the way they behave? What are some similarities and differences in the twins you know?

4. Describe a strange coincidence that has happened to you. Tell why it was unusual and how it made you feel.

Understanding the Book

The following questions are designed to assess students' understanding of important factual information after reading the book.

1. What was Charles Fort's last book, *Wild Talents,* about? *(Wild Talents was about human psychic powers, unexplained disappearances, and other mysteries.)*

2. Why is the mysterious force called the "cosmic joker" that is described in the book? *(This mysterious force is called the "cosmic joker" because it seems to have a sense of humor and to like to poke fun at us.)*

3. What fell from the sky onto a local school in Workingham, England, in December of 1974? *(Eggs fell from the sky onto the school.)*

4. What fell from the sky onto Mrs. Hiram Winchell's doorstep in Evansville, Indiana, on May 21, 1911? *(A young alligator fell on her doorstep.)*

5. What object did Sir Anthony Hopkins find at Leicester Square in London, which turned out to belong to author George Peifer? *(Sir Anthony Hopkins found Peifer's copy of* The Girl from Petrovka, *written by Peifer.)*

6. What coincidence was involved with the sinking of the Titanic? *(American writer Morgan Robertson had written a story titled Futility in which he describes the building of a great ocean liner named Titan and its sinking after hitting an iceberg off the American coast.)*

7. What happened to the coffin of actor Charles Francis Coghlan, who was buried in Galveston, Texas? *(The great hurricane which hit Galveston in September of 1900 swept his coffin out to sea, where it floated to Coghlan's home, Prince Edward Island.)*

8. What were some of the similarities between the twins known as "the two Jims" who had grown up apart? *(They both grew up with brothers named Larry and had dogs named Troy; both had been married twice, first to women named Linda and then to women named Betty; both had similar work histories; and both suffered from headaches and heart trouble.)*

Thinking Critically

The following questions have been developed to promote critical thinking.
There are no right or wrong answers to these questions.

1. Do you think it is true that you can get more out of life by focusing on one thing, rather than trying to do a bit of everything? Why or why not?
2. Where do you think the eggs, fish, and other strange things that have fallen from the sky came from? How do you think these events happened?
3. Do you think that James Rusk, author of a book about a kidnapping, had anything to do with the kidnapping of Patricia Hearst? Why or why not?
4. How would you explain twins who are separated at birth but grow up to live amazingly similar lives? Do you think it makes a difference if they are identical twins or not? Explain your thinking.
5. How do you think triplets and other multiple births compare to twins? Would you expect to see more similarities or more differences? Why?
6. Why do you think so many different cultures have stories about a trickster?

Writing and Extension Activities

Choose from among the following activities to enrich students' understanding of the book. You may wish to select separate activities for students of different abilities and interests or to assign an activity as a group project.

1. Encourage students to keep a journal of all the unusual stories they hear, see, or read in the news for a week. Have students share their favorite accounts with the class.
2. Suggest that students search their library's periodical index for stories about the relationship between twins. Have each student read one story and report on it to the class.
3. Encourage students to write a creative fictional story featuring their own trickster. Remind students that the point of the story should be a prank or unusual coincidence that the trickster plays on someone.
4. Suggest that students write a fictional news account of strange objects falling from the sky onto their home town. Remind students that their account should answer the questions who? what? when? where? and why?
5. Suggest that students use an encyclopedia or other resource to find out more about the assassinations of Presidents Lincoln and Kennedy. Have students share the similarities and differences with the class.
6. Ask students to write how they think their lives would be different if they had a twin. For students who are twins, have them write how their lives would be different without a twin.

Millennium Prophecies

Vocabulary

basis

architecture

prosperity

prediction

bubonic plague

nuclear warhead

computer program

alter

previous

radio reception

psychic

former

assassinate

trade agreement

communism

Summary

Many people think great changes will take place at the beginning of the year 2000, which begins a new millennium. For centuries people have made predictions about what the millennium will bring. Some people have predicted war and disaster, while others have predicted peace and happiness. Some people have made predictions using their psychic powers, and others base their predictions on measurements within the Great Pyramid, a code in the Bible, or the movements of the stars. Which of these predictions will come true? We will have to wait and see.

Background

What year is it? Are you sure? As civilizations have developed their own calendars, the methods of calculating the beginning dates and the length of years have varied greatly. Some calendars are based on the seasons of the sun, keeping the same summer, autumn, winter, and spring months each year. Other calendars are based on cycles of the moon, beginning on each new moon every 29 or 30 days, but these years are slightly shorter than four full seasons of the sun. To find more about calendars and the years they began, look for information in *Millennium Prophecies* or in an encyclopedia.

Tapping Prior Knowledge

The following questions are designed to be used before students read *Millennium Prophecies*. Students' responses will be based on their past experiences, opinions, or knowledge.

1. Brainstorm to make a list of what you know about calendars. Include what you know about different types of calendars, holidays of different cultures, length of years and months, or other information. Then compare your list with the list of a classmate.

2. Tell about something you have read that included a prediction about some event to come. How accurate did the prediction turn out to be?

3. What have you heard on television, or read in newspapers or magazines, about the decade of the 1990s? How is the decade described? Do people seem to focus more on its positive or negative characteristics?

4. What do you know about life at different times in history? How was life different? How was it the same?

Understanding the Book

The following questions are designed to assess students' understanding of important factual information after reading the book.

1. What calendars other than the Western calendar were mentioned in the book? *(Some people use the Jewish or Hindu calendars.)*

2. What true prediction made Nostradamus famous in his lifetime? *(Nostradamus correctly predicted the death of the French king, Henry II, in 1559.)*

3. What great disaster to come did some scientists predict based on the measurements of the galleries and chambers in the Great Pyramid? *(They predicted that the world would end midsummer 2045.)*

4. What did psychic Edgar Cayce predict for the U.S. in the years leading up to the millennium? *(Cayce predicted that there would be earthquakes in California, and that part of the state would fall into the sea; that disaster would hit the East Coast and New York City would disappear; and that there would be terrible floods in Mississippi, Missouri, and Louisiana.)*

5. What did Dr. Eliyahu Rips say he found written in code in the Torah? *(Rips says he found the names and the birth and death dates of 32 famous thinkers.)*

6. What sign of the zodiac will the Sun enter around March 23 of the new millennium? *(The sun will enter the sign of Aquarius.)*

7. What do most astrologers think the Age of Aquarius will be like? *(Most astrologers think the Age of Aquarius will be one of peace and greater understanding among humankind.)*

8. What did the prophecies of St. Malachy tell about? *(St. Malachy's prophecies told about all the Popes since 1143.)*

Thinking Critically

The following questions have been developed to promote critical thinking. There are no right or wrong answers to these questions.

1. How would you interpret one of the two quatrains of Nostradamus printed in the book?

2. Do you think that the builders of the Great Pyramid intended the measurements of their galleries and chambers to represent the dates of future events? Why or why not?

3. How do you explain Edgar Cayce's correct predictions of the stock market crash and the assassinations of Presidents Roosevelt and Kennedy?

4. Do you think it is possible to find hidden messages in any text, or are there special hidden messages in the Bible? Why do you think so?

5. What effect, if any, do you think the stars and planets affect events on the Earth? Explain your reasoning.

6. Do you think it is possible to tell a person's future from the lines in his or her hand? Tell why or why not.

7. Do you think it is possible for people to make accurate predictions about the future without using supernatural means such as psychic powers? Why or why not? If you think it is possible, tell how.

8. If the Bible does predict the future, why do you think these predictions were made?

Writing and Extension Activities

Choose from among the following activities to enrich students' understanding of the book. You may wish to select separate activities for students of different abilities and interests or to assign an activity as a group project.

1. Suggest that students write a story set in 2050. Make sure students include imaginary information about the time period such as world events, technology, and popular entertainment.

2. Have students make their own predictions for the new millennium. Ask them to write their predictions in lists and share them with the class.

3. Have students write an imaginary news report about the end of the world. Encourage students to share their news reports with the class.

4. Encourage students to use the keyword *millennium* to search their local library's periodical index. Have students read one of the articles they find and report what they learn to the class.

5. Suggest that students write a description of life in the 1990s to be read by people in the 2090s. Have students share their descriptions with the class.

6. Have students use American history books or other resources to find out what life was like in the 1890s. Encourage students to report their findings to the class.

7. Ask students to think about what they and members of their generation might do to make life in the new millennium better. Collect their plans for improving life on Earth in a notebook.

8. Encourage students to plan a ceremony marking the end of the millennium. Have students present their plans to the class.

Powers of the Mind

Vocabulary

You may wish to review these content words with students prior to assigning the book.

mental image

police commissioner

destination

architecture

cutlery

success rate

clergyman

botany

barrier

incident

vibration

pressure

chemical substance

docking module

Summary

Many people all over the world claim to have unusual powers. Some people claim to be able to see images in their minds of far-away things or to read minds. Others claim to be able to get information by holding an object or to find water by using a weighted thread. Still others claim to be able to bend or move objects with their minds. Parapsychologists study these claims, no one knows exactly how these powers might work.

Background

The human brain is constantly sending and receiving messages. The left side of the brain sends messages to the right side of the body, and the right side of the brain controls the left side of the body. A brain in a newborn baby weighs about one pound, and it is a fully-grown three pounds by the time a child is six years old. Scientists have studied many functions of the brain, the parts of the brain, and even the ways diet and exercise effect the brain, but there remain many mysteries. For example, scientists don't know why people dream, why some people can sense what is about to happen, or why some people seem to have psychic powers.

Tapping Prior Knowledge

The following questions are designed to be used before students read *Powers of the Mind*. Students' responses will be based on their past experiences, opinions, or knowledge.

1. Tell about a time when you have sensed what was going to happen, and then it really happened. Or describe a time when you and someone else said the same thing at the same time. How did it make you feel? Do you think these types of things happen by chance or because of a sixth sense?

2. Describe a book or article you have read about someone who claimed to have unusual powers. What did the people say they could do? Did you believe them? Why or why not?

3. Retell the plot of a movie you have seen about a child or adult with unusual powers. Was the movie supposed to be realistic just for fun?

4. Some illusionists make money conducting magic shows in which they seem to bend objects with their minds or seem to read the minds of the audience. Do you think all of these are just magic shows or are some real? Why do you think so?

Understanding the Book

The following questions are designed to assess students' understanding of important factual information after reading the book.

1. Why did some people believe Pearl Curran's claim that her poems, historical novels, and plays came to her as mental messages from a girl named Patience? *(Some people believed Pearl Curran couldn't have written the poems, historical novels, and plays because she had only a basic education and was not interested in history or literature.)*

2. How did Gerald Croiset help the Dutch police solve crimes or find missing people? *(Croiset used psychometry—he received mental images by holding an object associated with the crime or disappearance.)*

3. How did Dr. Richard Hodgson think Eusapia Palladino might have moved a table? *(Dr. Hodgson thought she might have used her foot to move it.)*

4. What did some television viewers say happened when they watched Uri Geller bend metal objects and stop and start clocks with his mind? *(Some television viewers said that cutlery in their homes was bent and that their stopped clocks were started.)*

5. How did Joe McMoneagle say he helped the CIA? *(McMoneagle says CIA members brought him documents or photos, and he used his remote viewing powers to find the person or get information.)*

6. How do ESP researchers make sure that people being tested are not accidentally signaled by others? *(ESP researchers put their subjects in separate rooms and use computers to choose the objects or pictures the subjects are trying to "see.")*

Thinking Critically

The following questions have been developed to promote critical thinking. There are no right or wrong answers to these questions.

1. Do you think it is possible for a person's mind to leave his or her body? Tell why or why not.

2. Discuss some ways in which you could accurately test a person's psychic abilities, without providing them any possible way to cheat.
3. From the information in the book, do you think Uri Geller, the man who bent spoons with his mind, was genuine or a fraud? Tell why you think so.
4. If it is true that people can affect dice and cards with their minds, how can games be played fairly? What rules might you make to guard against playing with psychic advantages?
5. How would you be able to tell if someone was using psychic powers to win a game?
6. Why do you think that people who believed in ESP scored higher in ESP tests than those who didn't?
7. Why do you think Hubert Pearce did better on ESP tests when he was given $100 for each correct answer?
8. Do you think psychic perceptions probably work more like sight, hearing, taste, touch, or smell? Why do you think so?

Writing and Extension Activities

Choose from among the following activities to enrich students' understanding of the book. You may wish to select separate activities for students of different abilities and interests or to assign an activity as a group project.

1. Encourage students to conduct an experiment in telepathy. Have one student sit at the back of the room and draw whatever comes into his or her mind on a sheet of paper. Have the rest of the class try to draw the same thing.
2. Have students write a brochure for a telephone psychic service or for office appointments with a psychic. Ask them to include ways they would convince others that the service was legitimate.
3. Encourage students to think of what psychic power they would most like to have. Suggest that they write a journal entry telling what one day would be like if they had that psychic power.
4. Suggest that students use index cards to make a Zaner pack. Then have a student shuffle the cards. Next, have the rest of the class write down the order of the cards. Have the first student write the real order on the board so the students can see how they did.
5. Suggest that students use the periodical index at their local library to find articles about the American Society for Psychical Research. Have students report their findings to the class.
6. Ask students to write a short story about what the world would be like if everyone could read each other's minds. Collect the stories in a notebook or binder.

Mysterious Healing

Vocabulary

electric shock

psychic

energy channel

infection

hypnotist

trance

telepathy

recovery

therapy

World War II

conventional

traditional

relaxation

diagnosis

numerous

Summary

People in all times and places have had ways other than Western medical practices of treating illness. Millions of men and women claim to have been helped by psychic healing, color therapy, psychic surgery, acupuncture, ayurveda, and iridology. Doctors know that many illnesses are psychosomatic, or related to the mind. Some people believe that those who practice other types of healing treat only the patient's mind, and that the mind cures the body.

Background

Traditional methods of medicine practiced in North America have included extensive training of doctors and scientifically tested treatments. For a person to become a medical doctor, he or she must successfully complete four years in college premedical education, four years in medical education, and three to seven years of specialized, supervised residency training as they work with patients. Some specializations include even more years of education and training. All of these years of training help doctors become experts in how your body works and how to keep it healthy.

Tapping Prior Knowledge

The following questions are designed to be used before students read *Mysterious Healing*. Students' responses will be based on their past experiences, opinions, or knowledge.

1. What are some methods a medical doctor uses to treat you when you are sick? How do those methods help you get well?

2. When you do not feel well, what are some things you do at home to help you feel better?

3. Tell about a television program, an article you have read, or a live show you have attended that involved someone who had healing powers. Did you find these powers believable? Why or why not?

4. Discuss what you know about the martial arts. What benefits do you think a person receives from these practices?

Understanding the Book

The following questions are designed to assess students' understanding of important factual information after reading the book.

1. How did Rose Gladden say she knew where to put her hand to cure Mr. Chapman's ulcer? *(Gladden said a little star appeared and floated over the place where the ulcer was.)*
2. How did Matthew Manning cure a patient of back pain? *(He imagined the pain as a red area, and imagined using a sponge to soak it up.)*
3. Why do doctors and scientists believe that psychic surgery is trickery? *(They believe it is trickery because they examined the blood and body parts that were claimed to be from patients, and found that they came from chickens or pigs.)*
4. How does acupuncture work? *(Acupuncture works by inserting needles into the skin and correcting the flow of the patient's chi.)*
5. What do Hindu teachers call a person's life force? *(Hindu teachers call the life force prana.)*
6. How did Semyon Davidovich Kirlian's photographs show changes in people's moods and health? *(The photographs showed changes in the colors, patterns of light, and brightness of people's auras.)*
7. How do iridologists see illness? *(Iridologists see illness by observing marks in a person's iris, the colored part of the eye.)*
8. What did Professor John Hasted claim that Matthew Manning was able to do in the laboratory? *(Hasted claimed that Manning was able to change the chemical makeup of a human enzyme that causes migraine headaches.)*

Thinking Critically

The following questions have been developed to promote critical thinking. There are no right or wrong answers to these questions.

1. How do you think visualizing (imagining) the disappearance of pain can help to relieve it?
2. Do you think it is possible for silver fillings or a rotten tooth to turn into gold? Why or why not?
3. Do you think that psychic surgery is a legitimate method of healing or that it is trickery? Explain your reasoning.

4. Professional magicians call themselves illusionists because they can create the appearance of magic by tricking what our eyes see. How might a magician's show compare to the shows performed by psychic healers?
5. How do you think relaxation exercises, such as those practiced in t'ai chi and yoga, help heal a person?
6. How do you think following the five rules of Reiki might prevent illness?
7. What are some ways you could use to find out if a person had really been healed by someone who claimed to have unusual powers?
8. Do you think that some illnesses might be psychosomatic, or caused by the mind? Why or why not?

Writing and Extension Activities

Choose from among the following activities to enrich students' understanding of the book. You may wish to select separate activities for students of different abilities and interests or to assign an activity as a group project.

1. Suggest that students experiment with plant growth. Plant similar seeds in two containers. Have students talk to one container of seeds each day, but not to the other container. Then have students record their findings of whether talking to the plants made any difference in how they grew.
2. Ask students to write articles about their favorite home remedies. Make sure they provide detailed instructions on how to use the remedy. Collect all the remedies in a notebook.
3. Encourage students to think about what it would be like if they could heal people just by thinking about them. Have students write a creative story about what one day as a psychic healer would be like.
4. Suggest that students write an account of a friend, family member, or other person who got better without help from doctors. Have students share their accounts with the class.
5. Ask students to write an essay supporting or opposing alternative forms of healing. Have students share their essays with the class.
6. Discuss with students the fact that different cultures have different traditional forms of healing. Encourage students to write articles about the traditional healing practices of their cultures. Have students share their articles with the class.
7. Suggest that students research health care professions in their local library. Ask students to choose one of the professions they find and read about it. Have students report their findings to the class.
8. Encourage students to find out whether there is an academy in their home town that teaches karate, aikido, t'ai chi, or yoga. Have one or two students visit or call the academy to find out more about these martial arts. Have them report their findings to the class.

Steck-Vaughn
Unsolved Mysteries

Alien Visitors and Abductions

The Bermuda Triangle

The Cosmic Joker

Ghosts of Flight 401

Giant Humanlike Beasts

Millennium Prophecies

Mysteries of the Ancients

The Mysteries of UFOs

Mysterious Healing

Powers of the Mind

Water Monsters

Where was Atlantis?

STECK-VAUGHN
C O M P A N Y

A Division of Harcourt Brace & Company

ISBN 0-7398-0097-3

90000

9 780739 800973